Darkling I Listen

AF664901

Chandraboli Ganguli

BookLeaf Publishing
India | USA | UK

Presentation by *BookLeaf Publishing*

Web: www.bookleafpub.com

E-mail: info@bookleafpub.com

ISBN:9789363306363

First edition 2024

To the Eternal Mother, Sree Sree Maa Anandamayee...

And to Lord Christ—my first confidante, and friend who taught me what it means to be human.

ACKNOWLEDGEMENT

To write an acknowledgement for a book of poems calls for acknowledging several generations of poets and authors without whom a seven-year-old me could never think of such a thing called a poem. Poetry knows no limit, and art knows no language. However, the poet who dug out my niche for me was, and will always remain my cousin, Arijit Mukherji, who died when I was six. I had probably seen him only when I was 4 or 5 years old. I can't recall his face, but I remember the chocolates he brought for me from the US. And I remember him scooping me right into his arms. Little did I know then, that he would be leaving behind his most valuable treasure for me to inherit. He left behind his book of poems, *The Young Magician and Other Poems*. He was the young magician who unwittingly shared the tricks of his trade with his little cousin. All she had to do was read.

My aunts, Chitralekha Bhattacharyya, Ruplekha Chatterjee, and Anuradha Mukherji (late) have probably been my earliest admirers, fanning my poetic fire, and making sure that the poet grows strong, and confident. Even when I wrote on unconventional or controversial topics, they lent a patient and unbiased hearing. My parents, and later my parents-in-law too, have been ever so enthusiastic to read my pieces, and though they often admitted to not understanding even the head or tail of them, they tried. With some classes from the poet herself, their hearts started beating to the mystic whisperings of the bard's heart.

My friends, Shraddha, Kashyapi, Ankita, Sangita, Tushnim, Kasturi, Shovan, Amrapali, Ajay and Anindya have always been the first in the line to receive each of my poems in their WhatsApp chat, at almost the same time when I put the last full stop in a poem, even if it is well past midnight. Thank you for not just reading, but for being my earliest critiques.

Lakshmi…the Sree of the monsoon—I could not thank you enough for coming up with the title of my book. You, Pushkar, Dr UmaSankar, Dr Laxmi Ramana—it is so difficult to digest the fact that you are all my colleagues…it feels like I have known you forever (not as colleagues though).

My dear Seemanti Miss who witnessed me grow, and Dr Anshuman Khanna, Dr Banibrata Mahanta, Dr Rahul Chaturvedi—your eyes always announce how proud you feel every time I write something.

Last, but never the least, my dear husband, Dr Kaustav Chatterjee—thank you for your sweet (though, sometimes not so sweet) admonitions to push me out of my comfort zone and share my work with the world. I know I am a tough nut to crack. Thank you for your keen ear despite sleepy eyes when I force you to listen to my recitations. Thank you for bearing with my "byaa"s and "boo"s, "mew"s and "grrr"s when the muse in me occasionally set out on a sabbatical, leaving my original self behind, until she returned. Thank you for all that you have done, and will most willingly continue to do, but most of all, thank you for just being there.

PREFACE

Since a very tender age, I have had episodes of defamiliarisation where everything around me looked new, looked strange—almost alien. This was long before I had any knowledge of Shklovsky and Russian Formalism. This sense of alienation drove me to put to words what I saw and felt, my childhood brain often finding it amusing to treat my writing as a cipher for hidden feelings and messages. I wrote poetry because I did not want to write a diary (In case I die young, or worse still, lose my diary).

In my initial days as a poet, when I was barely 10, a poem, for me, had to rhyme. I was in no way scholarly enough to read and understand metres, rhyme schemes or rhythm. I wrote. I do not know if I was any good, though. Initially, my act of defamiliarisation was accidental, later deliberate—to push me into a poetic trance, which could be triggered by something as trivial as a spot on a blank wall. I started frequenting a limbo from where I could get a view of both worlds—the so-called real, and the perceived. The more I alienated my mind from my surroundings—the more bizarre my thoughts became, and that was when I realised that I had become my own philosopher. My love for Kant, Camus, Kafka, Sartre, Baudelaire, Schopenhauer, Aurelius, Nietzsche, Heidegger was not born from what I got to learn from them, but from the kinship I felt with them upon learning that I was not alone—that I am not the first, and that I was not an alien, after all. I chose to study literature because I wanted to read more—I wanted to enrich my poetry. I started reading poems aloud, in full fervour, going an extra mile by imagining myself to be the poet who wrote the iconic pieces. I started looking through their eyes, focusing on the blind spots that their writing missed. My poems evolved, often becoming a rendition of my literary idols.

I can't predict my trajectory as a poet, nor can I foresee the meandering of my mind to explore the unexplored. I can, however, give myself the assurance to keep the poet in me alive for almost as long as I breathe. And after that, my books will live on. Even if in some forgotten corner of a quaint library, someday maybe, a someone or two will pick it up, flip through the pages, and smile…for someone has spoken their mind. They are not alone.

Reflections on a Keatsian Ode

In what reveries did the nightingale pour
In my ears its heavenly hymn?
That I, in a Keatsian ardour,
Drank the warm South filled to the brim.
Drunk! In an Elysian mirth,
I had once sung the happy ode.
Gone is that fervour, the nightingale has flown
Between the setting and rising sun, a dozen years scored.
And many a time I've found myself
In Keats' waking dream,
Falling half in love with an easeful death,
Afloat in the Lethe, upstream.

I've known what it's like to feel rich enough to
die…
Indeed, a child's romanticism at eighteen
when you wish to cease at twenty-five.
For twenty-five was a viable, die-able age,
And you've always wished to die young.
I'm thirty now, five years over twenty-five,
Holding on to life like I once held on to the
melody the nightingale had sung.

I'm still in love with an easeful death,
I've missed the ticket to twenty-five…
Christ was thirty-three
When he was crucified.

Feelings of death still loom large,
The insidious wish for an eternal sleep creeps in.
Yet alien is the feeling of being rich enough to
die,
With maturity growing fatter, eros goes thin.

The lure of death is romantic no more.
Was it me, that Clemence heard hitting the water
cold?
In the heart of Amsterdam and the seven circles
of hell,
Clemence's fall begins to unfold.

And yet, when I let my imagination wild,
I realise that the onlooker too was none but I—
Falling the infinite fall through the layers of hell,
Where death is the redeemer, and to live is to
die.

The Woolf's Howl

The moon glows so full
That its margin can't hold.
Spilling cross the sky,
The light's breaking the mould.
And even in its full-moon glare
The night remains cold,
Afraid of its waning,
The shrivelling, and the old.

And turning moon-ward
The weary Woolf lets out no howl;
A whimper at best,
A bemoaning growl.
The palsied grim-reaper slobbers,
Spittle and blood drooling from his jowl,
The Woolf attempts not to hide or run
When the senile reaper's on the prowl.

Her clock strikes almost sixty.
She might grow old before she dies,
Locked in the attic when she asked for a room
Breathing in an air of malaise.
An attic to shelter her brooding,
An attic for her madness to thrive
To love, and smother, and bother her,
Killing her by the moment, forcing her to
survive.

They pelt stones of amour,
Till she's stone-cold inside and out,
She then finally unlocks the lock,
And allays all her doubts.
To skip 'n sink like a skipping stone,
An embalming deluge undoing the drought…
The myriad waves soothe her to sleep,
Relieving her from her last maddening bout.

Marks and leagues into the depths fathomless
The currents wring her neck.
A final time she lets out a howl,
But the sound's lost in the wreck.
The full-moon spotlights the ruffled waves,
Adorning the water with starling flecks—
The sole witness of the dying Woolf
Bidding Adieu over the deserted deck.

The Gardener

I summon the past, the yesterdays, the late
With these very hands that tend and till,
Beneath the green, a brown interface
That succours the wailing skies until
I crack it open like a safety vault and
Plant in it the seeds of woe;
And rooted forever in this pain
Grows the mighty foliage of tomorrow.
A green cloud on a sodden stick
It's ever stranded beneath the lofty skies
Like a sage with an undeterred will
To walk the green mile of the enterprise,
To unearth from its womb, its nest, its grave
To know the known, the tale I tilled,
The land I cracked to fecundate
The earthly womb as the Father willed.

Frankenstein is Dead

Would you look at me, once again,
As I have looked at myself?
Perhaps for the first time
In the livid dark,
I caught myself staring back—
Glaring right into my soul, as if
My body were made of molten glass.

You told me not to look…
Not to stand before a mirror in the dark,
Yet, I transgressed, and stared on
Until the little puddle of light
From the window
Dissolved into the contours of my face,
Distorting it.

Only in the darkness the monster confides,
In the light, even from herself, she hydes.

And I saw myself, not as an artist,
Or a mother, or lover would have seen,
But as a monstrosity of an existence,
Created by some Frankenstein,
Putting together leftover spawn, and leftover
Clay, breathing into my lungs
His leftover breath.

And yet, something still was amiss,
Neither warmth of life, nor purpose.
I was alive, for life's sake alone.
Frankenstein stole the Franken essence
And poured into me the spirit
That burnt my innards
And charred my soul.

Her darkness heavy, in the blackhole she hid,
In light, unbearably light, her soul undid.

I am grotesque, ghastly, beguiled.
Too high for the base, too base for the high.
Far too angelic to eat, mate, and die…
Too bestial to be even the shadow of the divine.
You took me over the precipice
And let me fall
Granting me a sorry pair of waxen wings that
melt
In the heat of the fire that in me you installed.

If I were made by your hands,
In your shape, then you too,
My God, are no less a monster than I…
After all, Lucifer too was made
In the God's image, was given the Godly eye.
But the Father erred when he
Breathed into Lucifer his own Godly dreams.

Now existence twines like a thorned crown
round her head,
By dying she proclaimed, "My God is dead."

The Eternal Ferryman

I write this poem for you, each new letter.
And another star in heaven as palm leaves sway,
Like an ember, a spark in the gleaming heap of
coal,
In the sunset dark.

At Rishikesh, the water is green,
A bridge with thousand spans stands
And clumsily the pilgrims cross the vast
expanse.
But no pot of gold beneath... the water snores.

The river flows on.
Lewd green cacti rise,
Next a group of stones.
Hansel and Gretel sleep
On their own little boat.

Beside them stretched
In agony, Cordelia,
In sympathy, Ophelia.
As out of the caves
The water roars,
Pauses,
And is still.

At Rishikesh, the water is deep,
Deep and green, green but clear
Like some distant coral isle...
Watching the empire disintegrate.

And I have known the ways of nirvana.
The paths that Schopenhauer and Solomon and the Buddha showed.

You are formless like a river; your arms are thin.
You flow like a steam, like an ugly line, like a ditch...
Oh! I drown into this stream of darkness
And all is empty around me, silver splashes.

At Rishikesh, the sky will frown
Looking down from bearded clouds
That look down as they encroach
Until the river one night will spew its accumulated hate.

Immortality is a dive in the dark water,
Along a wrong path, a cul-de-sac without end,
Ripples of existence close around me,
Wring my neck.

The ferryman rows the boat..
He who knows it all, with the river humming
"OM"
Over and over, and over again... telling me it is I
who steer,
And I, the seer, understand not God and his
ways,
And yet I empathise... cup my hands in front of
his face
To catch the tear drop before it fell into the
waters in Rishikesh.

You are up from the sea? Perhaps.
And the stars glitter like sea salt in your hair
That is tangled as the seaweed knots
The sea wove around you. Let me spin
The light around each star into a web
And in the centre the tarantula dances
The deadly dance of temptation.
What lies in the centre?
In the empty orb-like black disc that stretches
Into your eyes, coming out of your mind?
Words, empty words, more words...
And still more words...

And across it all sails the eternal ferryman.

His Wife's Fall

The alarmed tower gongs the midnight bell.
The city's asleep, the sea's offshore;
Not a stir or flux of time behind the door,
Insidious night watches over the insentient
sentinel.

The nightly hours slumber on in the unperturbed
rand,
A cotton cover of furious fumes suffocates the
infant sun.
The door ajar, a drooling dock makes a silent run
Like a greedy tongue devouring the last morsels
of sand.

She walks past the guard, glaring ahead at the flight
In her night-gown and a flickering flame, like a ghost
Walking in her sleep—the possessed wife of the host
Starts to climb the stairs, beyond the blurring sight.

The spirit of the night sang a lullaby to all
'Cept her; clearing her dreaded way up the mortified tower.
No sleeping city, no mad king could bewitch her final hour
To stop or veil the sepulchral horror of her sanguine fall.

"Here's the smell of blood still. All the perfumes
Of Arabia will not sweeten this little hand."
A leap from the vaulting ambition into the deadly land
Stained the King with her illusive blood, prophesying his doom.

News of a Birth

A new cry was heard at the ghat today.
The man was called in. His work unattended,
He ran in, to smile at those closed eyes
And tiny fists...only the tiny chest moved
Like a recurring wave; a baby was born today.

The setting sun welcomed the new moon;
The fires raged on as they normally would,
The man came out, still wearing smiling eyes,
Adding more husk and wood to the fire;
Smashing the skull for an easy cremation.

Amidst the countless bodies stripped of life,
A new birth adorned the burning ghat.
He would burn bodies too when he grew up.
He would celebrate birth and death alike.
He too would wait for the news of birth amidst
death.

The Money-Jar

I chose a world for myself.
I chose to see with my eyes closed.
I chose to be mad.

Sometimes, only sometimes
Do we realise that we do not live in this world…
The world lives within us.
And you'll see that you've found all that you've lost—
—The innocence of the days bygone,
That I had shoved into a crack in the wall,
Like a child's money jar
So that no one could find it.
I know of that remorse when I realised
That even I had forgotten where I kept it.
How could I forget? How?
Years later, when I plunged within,

I found the same crack, the same treasure sack
Still beating behind the boney jail chambers.
The heart, like a ship afloat on the
Rhythmic waves of inhalations and exhalations.
Did I not find your face afloat, your
Hair wreathed with seafoam,
Like a merfolk
Chanting sad prayers—
—"Godspeed".
How would I know that you knew not how to
swim?
If only I knew what dreams are made of,
I would have told you not to dream because
Merfolk drown only in their dreams.

After a long spell of barren ink,
I have re-found how to spell my thoughts.

The Song of the Road

Long along the forest strand the roaring river sings,
Crunchy leaves beneath my feet speak of wondrous things.
Long way since I saw that face in helpless an abode
Yet come, let me sing to you the song of the road.

They lunged on and on through the forest trail,
Like lonely beasts enacting the Sisyphean tale.
Day and day out they sang that lonesome song
Of the old and alive days that were gone long.

Two roving posthumous souls, embodiment of a curse:
While one would walk, the other would lay dead in his hearse.
At dawn their journey starts, on his shoulder his dead mate
At dusk the dead would rise, his friend was now to be late.

At daybreak he would walk to the place where souls reside,
With the fall of the sun, the other feeling lost would return to the hide.
And every day, they'd walk to and fro carrying the other's load,
I have often heard them sing to me the song of the road.

"On and on I sing the journey song
To befriend us as we walk along...
One blind, the other too dead to see,
Oh! What fate has befallen me!
I look at his face, I know he is mine,
Upon his face the golden sun does shine.
We'll be there soon, in our world
In the farthest corner where death has hurled.
I know not the way, but I am sure to find
For the mind shall see when the eyes are blind.
One step and two, through the forest trail...

On my shoulder, my companion frail.
The sun is to set, I almost see the light
Through the lids that curtain my sight.
We are almost there, so it seems...
I say this to my weakening limbs.
I feel a stir, does my dead friend wake?
To the end of the journey then did we make?"

As soon as his friend did seem to rise,
Did he fall into a death-like surmise?

"Oh! What fear on his face do I see?
Oh! What strange place might this be?
Where in this world is our home to be found?
How do I make the journey homebound?
Is this the path on which the sun has bled?
Is this my way on which I shall tread?
On and on I sing the journey song
To befriend us as we walk along.
Oh! it's getting dark, I hardly can see...
How do I carry a man as dead as he?
I feel weak, my feet do tire,
But to our home, we do come near.
Deeply I breathe, though I hardly feel alive...
Through this journey home, I must strive.
The sun is to rise, a new tinge of red
To bathe me as I sleep on my tired bed.
At last, I think I see our home,
At last, I can cease to roam."

Saying this he fell into a fatal sleep,
The dead one rises, begins to weep.
The earthly home is no place for souls,
With his dead friend he begins to walk to his goal.
I have seen the two walking through day and night,
One moved to, the other away from light.
I have felt in my heart the utter despair,
As on their shoulder, the load of death they bear.
One was like the body burdened by the soul,
The other, the soul tied to a body, so cold.
Neither alive, nor dead, they knew not where to head,
Having different aims, they each had a separate path to tread.
Though they walked on every day, their journey never did end,
Like Sisyphus, this was their curse that they couldn't transcend.
While one loved earth, the other longed for the eternal abode,
Come let me sing to you their song of the road.

Dreaming the Omnipotent's Dream

The tea leaves have settled at the bottom of the pot
She counts the cards, stirs the spoon...
Through the sunset water, she divines her tomorrow.
Content to sleep unthreatened on the stone
And climb a ladder in her sleep
To where the pine needles opium stung
Droop down in languid dreams.

Stir the water anew, let's make some more tea
A cup of revived dreams for you and for me.

Clouds grow like moulds, like white-washed
moss
Hover in the silent thoughts and dreams
Waxing by strange moons, suffering losses,
screams.

But was *she* not a dream?
In the silent snores of dormant destiny,
The omnipotent dreams of you and of me...
The whole universe, just his dreamy play.
What if he wakes up?
Unweaving his nightly dreams in the light of the
day?

Oh, I have nightmares, nightmares in my
dream—
Teach me to dream of worlds that are bright
Float me into the sky quite free from strain
Kites in the sky try to be seagulls' shadows in
your pupils of night.

She has made up her mind, she has made up her
mind
And the bridge is ready.
All she must do is march across.
She has crossed the threshold and entered
The dark yet doorless room of someone else's
eyes

Leaving the drawbridge of the castle of your
mind
She screams, "Don't close someone else's door,
Open mine!"

How did the magician forget his spell
And lose control?
Maturity grows fatter every day.
When you thought you shook the earth,
Wisdom rocked you out
Spewing volcano-like into a new birth.

Stir the water anew, let's make some more tea,
A cup of revived dreams for you and for me.

Tomorrow when these visions will have gone,
Tomorrow when your eyes will take a slice
Of all the visions, when delusions will have
gone
When all these trivial things shall come to pass,
Tomorrow I will lunch with you upon the grass.

If You Find Me Dead

It's been more than a fortnight.
I have lost count of days, of hours.
No sounds of clock towers chime
Only the shells
Momentarily making me deaf.
At times I wish I could deafen myself
completely
But then your voice starts ringing...

I write letters, I don't know if you get them
At the shelter where I left you
About a fortnight back...
Son, when my embracing arms
Had to embrace the uniform of disgrace....
It must have been a fortnight...
Maybe more. I have lost count of days.

Birth is the greatest sin we ever commit...
Some days I wake up to find myself
Inextricably falling in love with death...
Some days your longing eyes
Shed a tear for me in my dreams...
Some days your mother smiles at me.
Maybe we'll meet her... soon.
Soon.

I left you something in your traveller bag.
Two. There are two bullets left.
If a telegram reaches you, don't believe I am dead.
Search for me...touch me, son. Embrace me.
Kiss me... kiss the nozzle
If you find me dead.
Pull the trigger if you find me dead.

Ideas

Letters and words
Filling up the silence captured in the white pages.
Years go by...
The blue fades, white becomes beige;
Yet neither warmth in heart,
Nor a smile.
Baleful eyes look around...
Incipient ideas lay in heaps
Crumbled up into ugly balls of rejection.

Once again, a new search through the old,
Scrutinised by the daunting eyes of existence.
Un-crumbling the balls...unravel-
Like an aging brown face divulging nascent thoughts
Into the nib of my pen anew.
I write again...with a new blue,
A new warmth, a new smile...
New letters making new words,
Resuming to make those ideas indelible.

The Moment of the Insider

Someone has knocked the fire out, the coal
And the cinders cover glowing, smouldering
coals
Like discreet veils, like smiles forlorn, like
patent leather soles.

All alone,
Yet not, but
Wrapped inside a feather swell…
All is gone now,
But that unknown stirring in the shell
A heart rich with memories,
Poor of souls—
Retreating, retreating into the deep cavern
Where one knows no riches
The distant tinkling of laughter
Like few five-cent coins
Rubbing their scent onto each other…
Those rich days with empty pockets!

A poor life stripped of love,
A poor soul huddled in the farthest corner,
Afraid of ridicule, of being alone:
A rugged heart wrapped in a shabby coat
Plodding ahead with the last remnants
Carefully tied into a carrier bag.

Could you not have waited just a moment?
In your haste you left the corpse behind,
And I, a leaf following in your hurricane wake,
Suddenly, fluttering, fell, to be trampled down.

Dead in this life, and dying in the after,
This poetry is alien to my ears.
Only poison,
Deep inside the moment
That has sustained,
Drains into one's consciousness.
Poison in the throat,
And poison in the eye
Only an everlasting poverty
Echoing in the poisoned rooms
Filled with poisoned memories.

Nirvana

With the last leaf, down came the last bit of life;
The earth lay still, shrouded in a cloak of dense
smoke,
And chilly air cutting through the glass surface
Of the motionless lake.
The day was falling out of the pupil of your eyes
Where the sun had stayed far, in a corner.
It hung over a precipice, and the clouds
Overcame it, clouds of night and doubt.
Could you ever have been alive?
The home to every being?
Could you once have been the keeper of life,
Who now is but a living carcass
Bereft of humanity?

Won't you wake up again?
To see the spring…?

Beyond that death where life lingers on,
Where birds sing cheerful songs, and the whispering wind
Breathes life back into you?
Up! Up from the grave, green velvet rolls down
Your rugged body to cover every inch
And dandelions sail on the impregnated wind
To every corner with the happy note of birth.
Stroll through the city that rises and falls
With your wondering breath, and heartbeat.

We have understood the ways of Nirvana.
Dying minute by minute, then being reborn.
Life springs from death… from frost to flowing springs;
A new spring… a metamorphosis
As the vernal spirit blesses the soul
To rekindle…to resurrect.

Waiting for Vladimir and Estragon

They came back everyday,
Or at least they thought they did;
They waited everyday for him to come,
But in fact, he never did.

Tomorrow, and tomorrow, and tomorrow yet again,
They waited for a tomorrow which never came...
On every tomorrow that sullen trick
Of disguising tomorrow in today's name.

Until one day, a sudden epiphanic click,
They had been doing it wrong all this while!
So they took a rope and swung it down
In an attempt to shun the base and vile.

They kept on trying it everyday,
With every tomorrow still failing them;
Now, waiting for Vladimir and Estragon
Stood Godot, who lives in the other realm.

The Narcissist

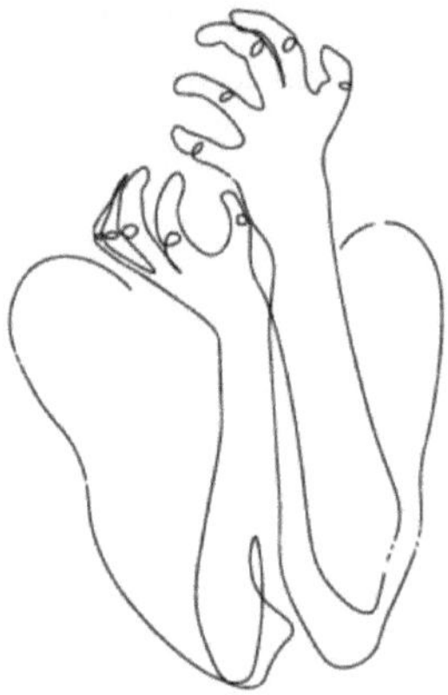

I am not my breasts.
Nor the crevice that you crave to look at
Like bloodhounds behind a closed brothel door.
I clench, dive deep into my body.
Beyond the soul—an outsider in my own glasshouse
Where I entered like a light beam, trapped forever.
I feel every contour, every dungeon
Moist with human sweat of hunger and lust.
The world thought I sinned.
I knew I was making love to myself.
When the world shunned the very premise
Of my existence, I turned to myself for comfort.
I loathed to see myself thus, I pitied what you rejected.

I carried myself like a lover in the midnight shower
Down, into the dark alley of shadows
And I showed myself what it was to live.

Darkness is all that I see.
Darkness that engulfed the light.
I have fallen in love with the darkness
Because it is infinite.
I have embraced my shadow.
I have plunged into the vast darkness
For when light fades...darkness lives on.
Call me self-obsessed. Call me a narcissist.
I tell you, I am on the quest to discover myself.
I am in there...somewhere I have given up
My search for an exit. I long to stay in here.
Immune.
Forever immune from the world outside,
Gently cradled to sleep in my own arms.
I shall kiss myself to sleep.
Freed from the shackles of bestial intercourse
I shall make love to life one last time.

I shall die of my bouts of schizophrenia.
That's a strange name they have given to my condition.
Doesn't schizophrenia sound more maddening
Than the actual madness?

I am inside a house in my dreams.
I am inside the house that I dreamt of.
Now that's all that shall remain.
A rugged skeleton with hollow eyes...blind.
Blind.
Air still flows through the nasal passages...
But the bricks shall fade. The veins shall melt.
All that will remain is the glasshouse and a
writhing soul
Trapped inside....finally dropped dead...for I
decided
That I would breathe no more.
That my heart would beat no more.
I froze the moment of ecstasy...an awe.
An awe in knowing myself for the very first
time.

Oh Captain of the Sinking Ship

"Oh Captain! My Captain, do I see the shore?
Oh Captain! My Captain, do we sail more?
Oh Captain, My Captain, with you as my guide,
I know I can sail on any tide."
"My boy, how do I tell you it's but a mirage?
These waters are notorious for delusion and sabotage.
How do I break it to you, that even with me at the helm,
We are cursed to be eternally stuck in this realm."

And did the captain have the heart
To tell you right at the start,
That to drown you were bound,
Long before you crowned,
And that from crib to grave,
you will holler and rave
Till the spectre takes you in its arms
And hums the holy Psalms,
Till you close your weary eyes,
Till when you'll never rise?

The wind rises, and with it rises the sail,
The captain sees right round the corner where
she's to fail,
Hold onto your dreams, or you will lose your
head,
Hold onto your heart as heavy as lead.
The heart sinks right through the ocean floor,
It sinks deeper, about 20,000 Leagues more,
Deeper and deeper into the Caldera's core
Where the earth bubbles the fuming gore.

Here's a good place to start forgetting
The knowledge that you gained when the sun's
setting
And forget as well, that this ship has been
leaking,

And you knew not for you were sleeping,
But if you'd listen, you'd hear the captain weeping,
For in your heart, she saw what you were seeking,
And she was afraid of your final bidding,
Where she knew, you'd sell your soul.

She'd sink with you to the very end,
And with you face, what destiny has penned,
And she'll soothe you of the horror and dread,
And she'll remind you that it's the same watery bed,
Where you rested whole months nine,
And cried and huffed when pushed out of the brine.

Covered in blistering barnacles blue, she'll sit with you at the bottom,
Till both have dissolved in the ocean's salt, forsaken, and forgotten.

Manimal Farm

No burden, no crime, no Lapsarian fall
Could unpronounce man's position as noblest of them all.
For man has said that man is right,
For man has claimed the gift of sight.
He has neither wings, nor talon, nor fang,
Yet the flight is his, the hunt, the harangue.
He is immune to neither fall, nor fire,
He'll die of venom less potent than his desire.
The Lion King is just a fable lame,
The lion in the hands of man is tame.
The ringmaster then turns to his son and quotes,
"Be as brave as a lion, as sure-footed as the goat.
Don't be a mule, be as strong as an ox,
As noble as the horse, if need be, as cunning as a fox,
As wise as an owl, as happy as a clam,
As slippery as an eel, as innocent as a lamb.

As graceful as a swan, as agile as a cat,
And to your father's folly, be as blind as a bat."

But if man's the best, why to animals compare
The virtue and vice of his noble heir?
For after the breeding, the birth, the feeding,
The heir is to carry out the man's bidding.
Not much different from crop or cattle,
The heir is to fight on the man's battle,
To take to glory Man's holy name,
And to carry on his back the forefathers' blame.
Multiplying in dozens to secure the bloodline,
And they dare to say it was God's design?
To birth them first, then subject to inevitable
slaughter.
Bit by bit die the sons and daughters
Like rats scurrying for the last drop to drink
On the deck of a ship that's doomed to sink.
Now rats hustle rats, the mice are caught in traps
Till the endless game ends, and their lifeline
snaps.
In the best interest of your heir, cease the
"harmless" harm,
It's time to bring to an end the mindless manimal
farm.

Weltschmerz

My day eclipses for a few seconds at eight
Soothing my leaden eyes
Heavy with ennui, and an inexplicable hate
For the sun which had to rise.
The darkness caresses my rocking head
Rattling against the speeding jail,
Allowing my eyes to open and see
The tar, and people marking the journey's trail.

In the darkness of the underbridge
Bathe the wife and her man
Rubbing off grime 'n dirt with a penny-worth
soap
That can't help their tan.
The darkness masks their shame,
As they rub, and rub, and rub.
They won't get any fairer, it's a lost game,
Only unfair means get you in the fairness club.

Give or take a minute or two,
At eight I see them both,
Scrubbing hard to get as close to clean,
'Neath the bridge hiding from the eyes of truth.
They aren't aware of my presence.
I pass by them too fast.
They are deliberately obscure 'bout the curious
eyes
In the yellow jail of iron and rust.

At 7:40 sharp I board the bus,
And walk a mile to the last window.
The heavy air of the day settles,
Pinning to the floor even my littlest toe.
I am paid to be my own jailor,
And institutionalise five hundred more.
Oh! Do I have it in me to cut loose
And thaw to life my core?

The Timemaker

There is a man trapped in a clock
Drawing the hands for the face.
His heart speaks in a tick and a tock
To create every minute and then erase
Until the clock runs out of time
And time runs out of a maker.
The clock announces the death without a chime
Forsaken without its keeper.

In Paddington station I have seen the man,
The accountant of minutes and hours,
An avant-garde art, which speaks more than
The man, and the clock he scoured.
Did we really try to tame time;
And lock it in a clock?
Could a stopwatch stop time in its prime;
And could hours go out of stock?

Do we dare trap eternity,
and set for it a paradigm?
Time lives us through our births and deaths,
And sets the universe to rhyme.

Darkling I Listen

Their world is different from mine.
Mine's behind a pane, marking
My home from the world.
The world is their home,
The world is theirs to roam.
They don't shy away.
They remind me of my first imagination of
Adam and Eve
Before their fall, before even the knowledge of
God.
We condemn them for not being us.
We condemn ourselves for not being them.
Primal—they live by their instincts,
Undocumented. They exist. Beyond a paper.
They have twelve. The oldest one
Nearly as old as I.
The thirteenth is in the womb.

Something in me stirs.
She won't live through her thirteenth.
The dead of the night breaks a new day.
Darkling I listen! to the recitation,
And repetition of words baking in the kiln.
Poetry is not for them. I make them my poetry.
Their chaos is my interlude.
Sometimes I can't tell my words from theirs,
Unable to tap the stream that disperses and
confluxes.
I want to share the burden of their chaos:
But what for them is trivial, hunches my back.
Amidst their chaos they sleep. I wake.
My senses flitting between the dream and the
deliberate,
I feel the shiver of goosebumps in awe of the
conjuring.
In the wee hours of another night, the thirteenth
is born,

And my philosophy, and my poetry.
Darkling I listen! Weak whimper of labour, the
newborn's cry.
My poetry predates my first
Browning, Tennyson, Wordsworth, and Keats,
Dickinson, sexton, Plath, and Yeats.

Unseaming

Gnawing bricks of incredulous intent
Haggardly with scaling shreds of a snake
A Gargantua eating through the soul
Burying in its gut the lonesome vagrant.
To touch the horizon and shatter it
Cut open the earth like nak'd mud-raked fields
To weave and unweave (g)olden pallid tales
—Drowsy city of bonsais and midgets.
Heritage, culture of scathing miseries
Of dislocated families buried deep
In pavement cracks. Put on a smile,
And wear some pride, make love to history.
        Rise, Oh Borough! discard the dream,
        stir a siege to
        Free Ganga caged behind the spokes of
        Howrah Bridge.

The First Marriage

Set the sky ablaze in the hue of dawn.
A shying moon stealthily moves aside
To usher in the soft sun-shrouded
In a red vastness tinted in the fresh paint of consummation.
The moon, still not out of sight
Smiles in her coyness as her whiteness glows
In the fire of vermillion sprinkled on her
By her heavenly counterpart.
The redness fades, her outline blurs.
Only the sun knows of her presence.
In the maturing hours of the aging sun
The world awaits in silence for the darkness.
Set the sky ablaze: the sun is dead.
Darkness must thrive.
The moon glows, like a tiny reflection
That her lover cast in her eyes unseen.
Only she knows that he still is present.

A brilliant glow of the widow shrouded
Speaking of words that once were his...
Her glow breaks the periphery and overflows the tide
to bring the sun back to life anew.
Storming red once again to usher in the
Renewed sun—the renewed passion,
Gently seducing the bemoaning moon.
The widow was a widow no more.
In your beginning is my end;
In your end my beginning.
And yet I live for those few moments
When you paint my forehead with your hue,
And internalise the pain of living in death,
And dying when alive,
Just to be betrothed to you over and over again,
Just to be smeared in the redness of your gentle touch.
Make love to me, oh spirit of dawn!

Petrichor

It creeps up my window and catches me in my
sleep.
Open-eyed, in a trance, I walk down to the place
Where intoxication fills every cell, runs through
every vein.

I splash around the mud like a child
Who has been instructed not to jump into
puddles.
It whispers unto me the news of marriage of
heaven and earth.

The clouds spread like a heavenly gown,
Like bridesmaids, make way for the groom to
meet the bride.
Longing eyes, shying smiles...and a hope for
unison.

Clouds roar, the drumbeats don’t stop, the play
of lights goes on.
It's a celebration of the eternal union of heaven
and earth,
While the fresh shower impregnates the earthly
wife.

It's the fresh scent of love, it's the musk of
arousal.
It's the wine of celebration which inebriates the
heart.
The lonely witness in the late hours of night.

It's a sigh of relief at the breaking of a dry spell
of an empty womb
It's the beaded forehead, the heavy breaths of
rest after creation of life
It's a news, it’s a nostalgia, it's a matchmaker, a
midwife.

It's a sedative...a magic spell to break all spells
of disbelief,
It's the roving spirit throwing pixie dust into
loveless rooms
Forcing even the least romantic to fall
inextricably in love.

Jigsaw Puzzle

Would you dream my dream?
Step into my body, into my soul,
So that you know that you
Are no different than I, and no different
Is your eye which sees, and lives, and loves
My dream tonight.
Would you walk up my road?
Take the backward step, and trip
Where I do, get up, brush your jeans
And continue to walk in reverse—in my
Feet, in my clothes, in my body
Walk down my memory lane.
Would you pick up pebbles for me?
One pebble a time. Time has smoothened
The rough edges so that they don't
Make my hands bleed—for my blood trickles
Down your veins. Would you pick up
Apiece, bits of the trail I left behind?

Would you look at the pebbles?
With my eyes, with my skin touching
The stones you picked? You'd know the stones
Were but bits of me that I lost, one step
At a time, as I dropped the last bit.
Could I go any further?
Would you put me back into a piece?
You found a heap of stones. Who'd know
They were once my bones? My soul.
The sculptor carved me fine. But how'd you
know?
The pieces don't fit anymore. They've worn out
So that your hands don't bleed.
Would you still try to fit in the pieces?
To make me whole; so, I could tread forth again?
You take the chisel, break a few pieces
To fit in the gaps the pebbles left.
The cracks still show, but the sculpture is good.
It wasn't even nearly me though.

You dreamt my dream, you treaded backwards
On the footprints I left behind, you picked up
The bits of a broken me, and put them together.
You saw with my eyes, felt with my skin,
You bled my blood. You had rebuilt
A *you* out of the broken me.

Painting a Portrait

Like a spoon diffusing the colour oozing out of
the teabag
I stir the sunset into the river with my finger.
Like the soft murmurs of the council of leaves
kissed by the wind,
Like the heartbeats of the squirrels who desert
not the deserted village,
Like the drop trickling down the window pane,
I try, with a million unnoticed strokes, to finish
the painting once again.

Paint a picture of the flame in the dark,
Bring to life the dead
Paint the scattered beams of the crescent - they
utter,
And the sword that's dripping red.

Like the strands of hair in front of the maiden's eyes
Moved by the breath of the lover at whom she blankly stares,
Like in the darkest night devoid of the hindrant cloud
Countless stars that appear...
Like each bristle that rustles on the canvas
To paint the artist's flare
Oh! the star, the ripple, the sword, the leaves
That I can paint not - I so despair.

Let me paint a portrait of you
The eyes, the nose the hair
And the lips parted in unsaid words...
To paint them can I dare?

Not the stars, but the night sky, the maiden instead of her hair,
Not the tears but the lonely eyes, and the Warfield nightmare.
I saw you as the broken bits, just the parts that made the whole...
The eyelashes, the smile, and on the right cheek that mole.
I can't paint, nor stories write when only the parts of you I see,
Not trees but meadows, rivers, not ripples and your serenity.

A portrait I had tried to paint, to capture you in a page...
Now that I know a landscape you are, in a fresh pursuit I engage.

Shall I Dig My Grave Tonight?

Shall I dig my grave tonight?
Beside yours...dissembling the dungeon wall,
I shall close my eyes and place
my hands where once your bones
withered away into dust and stone....
And I shall know anew what I had always known...
I shall hear your heart when mine would stop
For you were yet breathing in the breath
Of every being you dissolved into....
I breathed your breaths....and I'd continue still,
Outside that body that you've all known....
Fear not dears....for the blind seer

Has seen for us all what we tried and failed and
tried again yet to see...
I know I shan't die....
Oh then....oh...shall I dig my grave tonight?

Oblivion

The lingering waves, like a spectral frame,
The waves conveying your heartbeat,
Resonate in the darkening room
Of darkling spirits...
Like waning incense sticks.

Streaks of grey and white,
Sable lines of silver glide across
Showing every contour, every crease
Every greying strand
Like glowing hot lasers in the forbidden room.

Forbidden - there ends the journey thus,
I am forbidden from treading on your road,
Forbidden into the chambers echoing
Your heartbeats and your moribund smile
Evicted - from recognition into a memoryless
space.

Colours fade from my eyes
As they fade away from your whitewashed face,
Baptised after your youthful years,
To hold the star of nirvana, to chant names,
Not my name though...in that forbidden room.

I grapple through the dark,
Pushing away infinite sand dunes.
Bits of you torn away from my fists
Into a tornado of blackness,
Kissing the silvers black.

Oh, pluck out, pluck out these eyes of mine
Which could not see through the forbidden
mist...
Let these eyes not see
Which let you dissolve into an oblivion
Until the forbidden road is opened to me.

A Broken String

Withered tree, letting out two hands to reach up to the Lord,
Discoloured, almost lifeless, unable to hold on
Even to the last couple of browning shrivelled leaves.
A strong gush often comes with the news of death
But leaves to deliver the unwanted news to happy homes.

One day the wind brings along with it a friend.
A broken kite with a broken string,
Distraught: for having been separated
From the happy hand of the child,
Leaving him in tears.
The lonely hands
Of the leafless tree extends its soul
And holds the broken friend
With a mere thread to clasp.

Who held on to whom?
The wind kept on blowing
In its fury of having lost the kite
To the rugged tree.
Little did it know that the kite held on
Reminiscing the child's closed fist...
Or that the tree held on with a renewed hope...
Unable to give up the newly acquired friend,
Even in its last days, unable to say goodbye.

And they held on.
I never knew one broken string
Could be so strong.

Memory of a memory

I have often wandered around street corners,
Like roving spirits, like homeless ghosts:
I have lurked in and out those tinkling doors
Penniless, even to buy memories
From the memory store...

I have often seen my face on frosty windows,
I have felt your hands wiping me away...
And yet there I am again, as if never gone;
Like little fumes, like vapour droplets
You form by your own breath.

I have often seen you sleep in the rocking chair,
Singing to yourself that same lullaby...
I have seen you looking for me in old
photographs,
Gently stroking your fingers on empty spaces
Where you hoped to see me...

I have seen you fall in love with memories,
And pained when those memories did fade....
But I have often blamed myself for your plight,
For I am not the least a memory forgotten
But the lingering memory of ever having a
memory.

The Lost World

I have seen fireflies...
Amidst those fields and on the shore...
Amidst the wavering waves...
Their little lamps twinkling like souls.

I have seen fireflies...
Being born from the fire,
From the body lain at peace
On the pyre, the face ablaze.

Have I seen fireflies?
Were they not little parts of you...
An embodiment beyond your body?
Or memories afloat in the heavy air?

Far away, in little paper boats,
Flowers and a flickering flame set assail..

Going further away....like a tribute...or your
heartbeat...
Beating still....or so I willed...

I have held those fireflies
In my palms, like I once held your hands...
Oh! your warmth on that cold night...drying my
tears
And the greying itch in my hands...

Like the last flickering of the distant flames,
Like a sharp sliver piercing through the
darkness...
In the lonely night under the sleeping sun,
Wishing that may your fire forever burn.

The Hypnotist

The pair of eyes of a wilderness unknown,
Looking into me as if I were water
In a glass tumbler...
He spoke words which I thought I heard,
But indeed, I felt the words through my
deafness.

A twirling grey dancing round the bullet black...
Like a smokey planet in the ellipse red...
And I lay on the table top,
Breathing, sullen and slow: in a limbo
Stranger to both the living and the dead.

Tick tock...tick tock...
My eyes transfixed on the wall clock,
Staring- staring and drowning in the vast abyss
Voices like a psychedelic rendering...
And a cry: a howling rendition.

Awareness doesn't come quick...
Sitting in the dark room, staring into the stranger's eyes,
I see a reflection of a stranger me,
Regressing into the past, some other world maybe...
Or the faint outline of a three-eyed deity.

A Wicked Queen No More

She held out a looking glass;
"mirror, mirror, on the wall,
Who is the fairest of them all?"
She waited, heaved a sigh...
Restless within, she couldn't deny..
Nevertheless...she was still.
But
She breathed.
Her breath kissed the mirror,
Her vision was a blur;
The looking glass could show no more
Than an outline, bemist,
Of the damsel frenzied.

She smiled.
It was a looking glass after all...
Though the image in it she couldn't recall

It must have been her...
Yet she knew not
Those eyes, those lips curved in a smile demure.

Her soft breath was the truth.
The blurred image was none but
She, as she saw herself.
She needed not the world to say,
Or condemn her illusions away...
Spite the mist, clear was her smile.

And
The seven dwarves returned to their nest,
The Princess slept on her dreamy rest.
Neither the rose red, nor snow white,
But a sunny pink glowed on her cheek;
As upon the night dawn befell
Brothers Grim(m) had one story less to tell.

Read me through my silence

Read me through my silence...
The myriad thoughts storming in the poet's mind,
Closed until someone with the key to her heart comes
And unearths the treasures buried in the ruins of misunderstanding.

A conversation of vibes and connections in that utter silence...
Not a smile on their faces,
But the madman's laughter raging behind the curtains...

And once you've read her thoughts...
Your eyes twitch...in a silent smile,
Without any movement of lips,
Love flowing through the eyes which never could fade from memory...

That smile of empathy...of understanding...of compassion...
For now, you know, we are comrades set sail on the same journey.

City of Lights

City of lights, of lies, of lust:
Don't you allude to those days
Which I have seen engraved
In those stony crusts,
Imprinted in those grey eyes,
Those wrinkled leaves;
Telling us stories of the day
Before yesterday?

City of lights, of languishing lores:
Why stand in the sun
When bathed in fog and gore
Of the squirming millions
Buried alive in your stone-cold heart;
Those ghastly voices whispering,
Spite your deafness,
Of distant smiles of the day
Before yesterday?

City of lights, of loonies, of loners:
Why do you, like a ravenous snake,
Devour every vein, every soul,
Seeping through the graves;
Kiss the dead to wake up in
Your shadow, with poisoned
Memories and reddened eyes,
With no more to say
Of the glories of the day
Before yesterday?

Hues of the Thought Fox

They take pride in their hunting,
They mark all territories as theirs,
What can’t be tamed will be maimed,
They are the soul slayers.
Feed them the aura, feed them the verse,
Feed them the emotions, lift their curse.
Starve yourself, lest you steal their bread
They’ll thieve your brain for their head.

No! Don’t hunt the Thought Fox,
It’s not for you to tame,
Wait and watch if by you it docks
And nestles in your brain.

Else in the wild let it roam,
With its scurrying feet and timid paws,
Waiting behind the bush to trap its prey,
And trespass his thoughts where it slowly flays

His notions, and postulations, and convictions
away
Till the Thought Fox hijacks his mind,
With a gnawing obsession sprawling
Across his existence, leaving all else
In a void.

The Burning

I burn to liberate
I am the fire emanating from your soul.
I lie on the pyre.

With closed eyes I
Lie still, letting the flames
Afflict me.

I sacrifice myself for the sake of the child
I housed within me till now.

They call me dead—
A dead body.

I call myself the eternal—
With the ashes of triumph, I
Mark eternity on thy volatile forehead

I become one with the Lord.
I become one with the Earth.
I am the keeper of the soul.

Lord of the Rings

Jump through the hoops of fire-
A mere game I plot.
Jump....jump. Jump hard
That the fire touches you not.
Look here—you tiger-eyed beast,
You were born for this game.
One hoop after another...
You're a slave by the tiger's name.
I am the ringmaster, the sorcerer
Your cry, subdued by your fiery roar...
Jump till your roaring blurs
And you can jump no more.
The fiery rings then strengthen tight
Round your vulnerable throat,
I watch in glee as you fight
to get across the moat.
Tighter and tighter goes the hangman's noose
Burning you alive
A mere game that I set loose
To kill the tiger like a fly.

The Backstage Eyes

Hush! it's about to begin.
"Make way"..."Move aside".
The music plays...the choir starts the song.
The audience listens with rapt attention.
Songs of joy...of agony
To touch their hearts,
To strike the chords of the lute.
Feet tap, dancers swirl.
Feather toed in their dazzling gowns.
Applauds, and cheer.
Hush...it's not yet over.
Enters the ensemble of belles and beaus,
Playing stories of Juliets and Romeos.
Eyes transfixed on the story that's staged;
More claps, more cheer—immense grace.

A glorious evening—a magnificent show!
All rise, preparing to go.

Went unnoticed two lonely eyes:
Behind the curtains, obscure from sight,
Visible only in the empty hall,
To build the stage, to fix the light;
To see through an artist's orb,
To make, to create—to set the show.
Hush...it's about to begin.
Shove off the stage.
For, at the performers, people fix their gaze.
Two eyes in protruding sockets,
Like eyed white balls in the dark;
Sometimes a tear, at times a smile;
But alone. No one to speak to.
No one to know
The hands, the hard work behind the show.
Repelling spotlights, waiting in the far corner,
To unset, to undo after the show's over.

The eyes, so used to the darkness—
Comfortably immune to the nonrecognition.
To cast the light, yet never stand 'neath it.
A helpless smile, some abandoned tears,
Deaf to the sounds of claps and cheers.
As the performers and audience see each other,
They are all observed by a silent another.
And when one sudden day, the lights turn to see

The lonely eyes in the dark corner,
They can no longer bear the glare:
The spotlight is too strong—blinding.
The eyes close, a surging angst:
A feeling unknown hitherto.
The claps piercing through the eardrums.
Silenced cries of the lonely eyes in the dark
That dissolved into nothingness,
Unable to cope, to swim in that beamful deluge.

Bound and Unbound

"I say...come to me,
To me, to the very depth of thy soul,
Let me take thee
Away...away from the worldly rigmarole,
Come...come and embrace me..."

I hear voices, voices that allure...
I do not know if I quite like them,
But I'm helpless, without cure.
I take the leash of my mind, the rootless stem
It's to them to paint bold strokes defining my mure.

"Come....come hither thou must...
I will show thee; beyond the stars,
Beyond the senses, the precincts of love or lust.
I'll free thee from the fetters of this tragic farce
Where to live is to be iron bathed in rust."

I begin to gradually like the voice I hear...
It's one voice, a female's. Eerie...but nice.
Fearless, yet induces a tint of fear.
It's...it's assertive, but, free from vice,
Coiling the string of connection, to draw me near.

But then... I hear other voices too.
Less humane, haply more human, voices in chains,
Summoning me, trying to spread a smile or two,
With mortal blood traversing in their veins...
Sweet words they speak, but hardly true...

I shun the voices...I try to run away.
Madness isn't quite an acceptable word I guess,
But the mysterious voice finds its way,
Into my brain, permeating through my flesh,
To enchant me more by the night and day.

"I whisper, I whisper in thy mind,
Take one step, then another, and another.
Walk straight ahead, don't turn behind,
Let no wind or wave take control of thy rudder,
At the end of the dark tunnel, light thou shall find."

I succumb to that strange whisper...
I prepare myself for the journey,
My vision gets blurred...
Is it a tear? Or the wind harpooning my face?
Probably a bit of both...I infer.

I see...I see the light.
I... I hear voices too...uh...no!
I hear only one voice now, the others have died down,
Amidst all my moonshine talk...
That friend...who talked me to the door!

To The Voice of God

Days before the final sunset,
Dying dreams lurking on the bed-posts
Her eyes half closed, responding
To not a voice..
Doctors said, "Her life is in threat".
Reality was too unreal...a mere ghost,
That waited to be the spectral being,
Away from the babbling and noise.

She was still. As if by a catatonic seizure
Lost in meditation...eyes that did pray....
Oh! Was she a statue? Mere stone??
Or one shrouded in white, like regal marble?
Her relatives were busy! It was all for her.
Running here and there as the hours waned
away...
She knew...she waited for her life to be gone...
But in her eyes, they missed the glint...the
coming of a marvel.

They paid no attention to the faint smile
That played on her face through the oxygen mask...
They heard it not when she murmured...
A voice spoke to her...she felt.
A voice so tender...to lead, not to beguile...
"Whose voice was it?"...she tried to ask...
In the hospital suit, she slightly stirred
She was in another world...not where she dwelt.

She felt the lightness in her body...
The elevation was steady, but slow.
Like a spectral twin she did rise,
Leaving the bed...the room...the earthly light.
She looked down...and still there she slept
With stony eyes and a stone-cold chest.
But her face bore the smile she never saw.
"Did I ever look so beautiful in the mirror??"

There....she heard that voice again...
Magical...enchanting....alluring...
"In the mirror you smiled for yourself...
For your eyes to judge your joy...
But now as you smile, you smile for me,
Your eyes for me do search.
Your ears ring to my voice, dear,
In your transcended dream...it's now that you rejoice."

"But they are all crying," cried out she,
"They say I am to die...that
I don't deserve to see heaven so soon...
Yet I can understand not the chaos..."
The voice tolled again to her ghastly ears,
"They all will die too, that's known...
Life is but a bubble, dear...with lustrous baits
Guiling people along...."

She looked down again to her earthly self,
They knew not she was gone...
They were so busy with the paraphernalia of death
That they knew not what it was to die.
The voice unto her again spake,
"You bore a heart so pure,
Come with me to the other realm,
Where clocks don't chime, and a suffering unknown."

"Heaven....hell-- I heard them say,
What strange terms are these?"
"Earthly perceptions and penitence, dear,
That they too cannot perceive.
But in fear of damnation, these worlds they make
And act according to their own will"
This is what the voice did speak
And the earthly voices all became bleak...

Her heart ceased to pump, her pulses did not beat,
"She is no more," the doctor said,
Her relatives were all in disbelief.
Yet now they noticed the smile, that on her face did shine,
"Oh! Poor soul," cried one of them...
At your own grief you do smile....
And why wouldn't you?? You were ignorant...
Oh! What will she know of death?? She was only nine..."

I Shall Die Another Day

Dreams....I had them too,
I negotiate with myself...
Marking out my life with ticks and crosses.
More ticks, I stay.
More crosses, I.. 'ouch'
I tie the knot wrong. Again...
As the harsh jute rope
Cuts through my fingers.

I try....I keep on trying.
I cannot just get it right.
I go out to seek help...
I walk through the woods.
I walk alone till
I reach the riverside.

Staring at the black water,
Like the vast expanse of one death-trap alluring me,
I realise—maybe I do not need the noose after all.

I throw a stone into that blackness.
Like a heavy heart, the stone sinks.
An initial splash and sift...
Till the ripples clasp close
Like the pangs of existence
Closing the neck like a hangman's noose.

A cry—not mine, I say.
....Then....whose?
I look around....a little boy,
Frantically throwing his clenched fists...
As an attempt to slow his drowning.
I look into my hands...
The piece of jute rope
That savoured on my flesh and blood
Saved the child.

As he loosened his fist,
In it I saw the stone.
"I thought you threw away something precious"...
Said he, giving me the stone.
"And....thank you sire, for saving me."

I had tears in my eyes....
I closed my palms around his little hands.
"Why did you throw it, sire? It could have got lost..."
Maybe I did not want it to be found...until you found it.
Maybe I wanted to die.
"Well....don't give up, you can die now."
Never mind, child, I said.
Another day....I shall die another day.

A Mountain Lore

Tranquil—the mirror lay flat on your bosom...
Reflecting....enamoured by your beauty, O mother;
Each breath you take forming a beguiling mist,
A momentary shroud on the crystal clarity...

You look down intently, following every line
That defines your rugged female body; O mother—
Thy wisdom painted in the white and silver,
And shimmer gliding down the caverns of thy breasts.

The pain and sudor beading your cold temples,
Shuddering in the pain to give life...O mother!
But had you noticed those tears misting thy face,
In your lap lay cradled the stillborn life...

Clad in your white gown, an ethereal beauty--
Too huge to appreciate...your magnanimity, O mother,
A repelling attraction, a maze of cuts and ridges,
Like abrupt pleats of your frilly attire.

Your cold breath sending ripples across the mirrory lake,
Quavering the unmovable being, hallowed by clouds, O mother!
Your ancient enormity, my human gaze from thy foot
Unable to trace upward, no higher than your bust...

I was born at your feet...I needed to be suckled,
I wanted to be in your lap....O mother,
But purged and perished in your arms instead...
Still waiting for thy blessing...O Himalaya...My Mother!

And Time Stops....Only for You...

For dreams, for days...that count on fingers,
For the years which go by before we sway,
For memories that fade, but ever do linger...
And all good wishes condensed to this very day.

For eyes that sparkle and embellish the soul,
For stars that glitter like sea-salt in your hair,
For the smile like a gentle crease on peach-tint silk:
For goodness that inspires our sweetest prayers...

And time's sphere flattened into a looking glass:
The body on one side, on the other, the soul,
Behold with longing eyes and a wistful smile
Your yesterdays reanimated, to make your today whole.

Reflections we are of the young girl's studious
days,
Looking up to the mentor's guidance and care...
Clinging on to you, incomplete and pained...
Till enlivened by your touch, so magical and
fair...

For days that count on fingertips yet countless
be the years,
Let your joys not count on sadness and
happiness stream through tears.
Let your indomitable spirit enlighten the path on
which you tread,
Let your love whiten the darkest coal and you
say...
"OH DARKNESS! THOU MUST WAIT."

Let the looking-glass vanish and hourglass fail,
And we unite in this timeless sphere...
May your heartbeat melodise our days,
May time be frozen here.

Whispered Thus the Wind

The night wind whirls in the sky and sings
As evening melted like a sugar cube in a coffee cup...
Myriad stars...a partridge with spread-out wings;
A stray cloud stirring the azure realm...
A voice...like a song...the whistling of the wind,
Moonbeams peeping through the corniced pane...

'Neath the stars, the gurgling strand;
A bird calling out...madly in love
With the nocturnal disc, an occasional breeze
Fluttering through the maiden's hair...
Veliferous...like the sails of the homeward ship,
Gazing intently...the shimmering orbs reflecting in her glass eyes..

The wind, she heard, whispered into her spectral
ears...
Like a guardian...like Alladin's Magic Carpet...
Singing old songs...ones of her childhood;
A flashing thunder...like a creak in the grave,
Reminding of the crooked path to the land of the
dead...
An arpeggio on her spectral harp..playing the
symphony of silence..

A princcss...in her Athenian gown...
Seated on the partridge; guarding the Milky
Way...
Breathing a ghastly breath down the throat
Of some lonely gazer, lost in imagination...
Feeling the breeze....unaware, unperturbed
By the spiritual intervention....

In the sky shone silver the smiling disc,
In harmony with her unnumbered starry kins...
Casting a motherly look...like mellow
heartbeats,
At the princess and her winged mate...
Up they flew...and upward still to reach out...
To sleep in the arched arms of her heavenly
mother...

The maiden hummed...reliving the earthly dimension,
Pirouetting in her robe, like bubbles in a wine glass...
A diadem of fireflies haloing her angelic head;
Flying back home to kiss the moon...
Her lingering voice, heard...but unseen by the earthlings...
They thought it was just the night wind.

A Glassful of Memories

The corner table in the country pub
Seemed to be the only friend
As I witnessed the clock hurling the eve
Into the dungeons of the darkling end.
A flickering candle glowed in front of me
Casting a quavering pool of luminescence,
Outlining about half of my worn-out face
And warming my numbing visual sense;
In my palms I cupped my glass of beer,
With bubbles gliding in a clockwise twirl:
The gentle ripples kissing the class edge
Like the lemonade frills of the dancing girl.
On the table there stood a ceramic vase
And a thorned rose bathed in the colour of
blood,
Writhing in pain as if yearning for rest
In the bosom of its soft bed of mud...
I watched and I gazed into the chilling drink

Recollecting memories of the loving thee,
Avoiding to cast an occasional glance
At the surly empty chair sitting in front of me.

In the glass reflecting my sleepless nights,
A blurring vision 'spite the candlelight....
Like thawing memories touched by the blazing flame,
Water droplets on the glass, writing a nameless name.
Soaked my eyelashes an escaping tear:
A pinch of salt dissolved in my warming beer...
I recollect the ephemeral tenderness of your eye...
The hurting resonance of the unsaid goodbye.
Regaining my senses, I hear the music play
And a buzzing cheer of love-talk that the lovers say.
Dancers jigged to retro beats, lost was I in retro thoughts
Like the spreading ink stain on a paper that blots...
Like the empty nest waiting for the inhabitant to return,
The empty soul witnessing each day, the setting sun....
Craving for inebriation from that glass of drink,
The candle now flickering like eyes that blink...

As the candle blew out, it was darkness I stared at,
In that crowded tavern, lonesome I sat...
Into a whizzing intoxication my mind thus sank,
A glassful of memories from my tumbler I drank.

A Homeless Soul

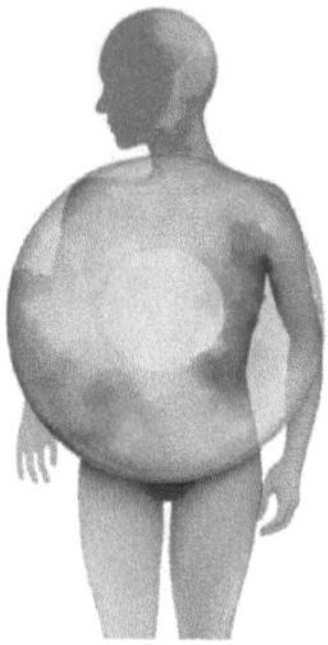

Through the two open casements
Entering the body…to reflect in the eyes…
Moonlight crept in to gleam on your skin,
To hug thee like an immortal kin,
As the head rested on the sleep-deprived pillow
In the womb of the lonely night…

Smoke filling the grooves of the brain:
Its cracked labyrinth reminding of some lane
On which the dead are said to tread…
And visible to the inward eye
A traveler lost inside a deserted body:
A soul ravished by an embodied mirage.

The traveler sitting by the orphaned strand…
Arising from the depths of the earth
Instead of great mountainous heights,
Dying in itself…like a body dissolved in the soul,

Squirming in the flood of tears and blood,
The spirit coffined inside the living corpse.

Poetry: An Appalling Beauty

Of words, of minds, of what senses speak...
Of joy? Or of pain? Or the iridescent streak...
What moments were those to wield the pen??
A countdown or an ascent..from one to ten...
Like the clawed hands of the beauty in black...
Of hideous smiles in pain....alack...
Like the sharer of secrets?? Of guilt?? Of love??
Passing moments with a cigar in some county
trove..

What dreams?? What hopes? Of what blinding
pain?
And calming vibes that do drive us insane...
An appalling beauty...to create and then to break
The nostalgia and inebriation like the ripples of
a lake...
Reflecting dreams and yet shaking them across..

Making one daydream, then pointing forth the
loss...
Stealthily entering the mind in the form of a
dream...
To weave the fabric of hope..then
shatter...unseam...

Like stories of saints...like heaven and hell...
With all the knowledge that one ever could tell..
Like insidious venom, like the psychedelic cry...
Like contingent imaginings, like a relieved
sigh...
To reave and bereave the poet's restless soul...
To make yet mar...and still, making him whole...
Revels...yet reveals...like time's truthful eye...
The likeness to life...yet making him worthy to
die...

A River Incarnadine

In a vast abyss...an empty space
Swirled nature to paint thy face...
Rocks cracked and crumbled down,
Soil weaving human skin vast and brown..
Volcanoes surged and bubbled in rage...
The fire in the soul, in the body it's caged..
Mother Nature opened out her arms...
Ornamenting the human, making him warm.
The whispering winds cast their magic too...
An inspiration to blow out and in the nostrils
two...
Finally the mountains melted, skies did cry
Through the veins watering the body so dry
Humans were formed...humans did live
More than peace, in wars they believed...
The water, salty with the tears of thee

Could not stop the war between you and me..
On the banks of the dried river, we warred
Striking the sword on all...whom we adored...
Breaths fled...lives bereaved...the water mixed
with soil
Iron strengthened the placid water in that turmoil
The redness did flow in front of the human eyes
Strewed with carcasses that the war did surmise..
The war did end and so did the human bond
With the rising sun, a new day dawned...
Shining helplessly on the river of blood..
To replace water with the veins of this flood...
Now blood flowed and kinship revived..
A new start...?? Rendering new meaning to
being alive??
I looked into your still eyes…unmoved by life..
My own breath cutting through my heart like a
knife..
Why didn't I value thy tears, O brother of mine!
Before you eternally dissolved in this river,
incarnadine..??

En-Graved

She was en-graved in her desolate grave
Beneath the starling night, so still....
As I fought against my very human crave
To dissolve the truth, to live my will.
And in a tempest to separate the living and dead,
Lord, you designed my destined way...
And that vision of her fiery bed
Badly pricks my heart even today.
That burning love, that unquenched wish
And the tormenting flow of blood and tears
Could not make my destiny unleash
My life, even in my dwindling years.

> Let me live, let those palm lines of destiny be gone,
> Lord, I pray, let me write my own in the years to come.....

A Maze

Oh what sorrows were those that the blinded eyes failed to see?
In taverns and empty nests...or kites hanging on to trees...
The lonely traveler in a desert who perished and nobody knew..
Or the cold North wind that from the depths of sorrow blew..
The mother who looked into the closed eyes of her stillborn child,
Or the snapped bond of lovers that was never reconciled...
The child with broken trust, for Santa Claus was not real...
Or the pilgrim goers whose train got derailed...
The busy man who never heard the cuckoo sing,

Or the maiden who was widowed on the day she wore the ring..
The fluttering butterfly whose wings got trapped in a hinge,
Or the death of the gory hen prepared to be singed...
The dreams and wishes that remained locked up in the heart..
Or the budding plant with uprooted life for a greedy man's sart.
The longing for love of a child whose mother died from childbirth..
Or wailing tears which dried in the eyes, concealed by a mask of mirth..

And yet, what about the sleeping eyes overlooking the drops of joy??
In horizons and smiling eyes...of satisfaction and foy..
The child whose boat in a rainwater puddle heartily did sail...
Or the aimless cloud happily drifting in the sky leaving a cottony trail..
The father whose little girl uttered "Pappa" for the first time..
Or the grandfather's clock which after long years did chime...
The poor man who in the morning dew saw diamonds gleam...

Or the herons who glided on the ripples of the stream....
The childless woman holding her dream child to her breast to suckle..
Or a long forgotten love-letter, read and unfolded, which had ruckled..
The beggar girl who saw a bit of the universe through her roof that leaked..
Or hopes of a child by the wishing well when life seemed bleak..
The busy bee that impregnates flowers and yet is unaware...
Or the lover who in the rising dawn at his sleeping love does stare..
The poet who sees surging oceans in skies....and the sky in the tranquil lake..
Or in the draughted land, the first drops of rain when dark clouds quake...

Like dandelion seeds floating in millions with the wind...
Like God blessing his children repenting after they sinned...
Like the aging mother smiling a goodbye to her boy who'd never return,
Like the raging fire which in its own flames seethed and got burnt..
Like the rainbow with its iridescence, indeed so ephemeral...

Like the river of blood into which the war-flag was furled..
Blinded eyes to open...and sleeping eyes to see
The timeless drops of sorrow and joys of eternity...
The wefts of sorrow and warps of joy, framing the grid...
In the fabric of life, intricate knots yet the ends are freed...
Hurdles and barricades, yet gateways and wings...
The play of 'MAYA' and the surprises it brings....
A labyrinth leading us to our final destination...
For some it's life, for some death...or God's condonation...
What would you call this life other than a maze??
Of miseries and miracles...simply to amaze....

I

I....
I am the question,
I am the I
That dwells deep down in your conscience.
I am an I,
An 'I' to make thee strong.
I am that I
Which loves thee more than I,
I am the I
Which assimilated with the I of yours.

I am an isle,
An isle to shelter thee in a flood.
I am the cosmic eye,
An eye for you to view yourself.
I am a fear:

A permanent fear in thy virile soul.
I am an identity,
The identity your ego denies.

I am the music...
The melody of your heartbeat,
I am the smile,
That shines on the face of mankind.
I am the light, I am the shadow...
I am the whispering wind;
I breathe fire and ice...
I am a glimmer
Shining through the darkest dark...
I am an era...a revolution.

I am a fire,
The fire of indignance.
I am the mother:
I create, I destroy...and I re-create.
I am an I, I am every I,
I carry the world in my womb,
I clasp the globe to my bosom.
I shudder in pain, I wail...
I dance in my inebriation.
I am the rhythm of life....
I am an I.

I am
A woman.

The World Beyond Death

Beyond what does the darkness strive?
To what limit may insanity drive??
Is death just the reverse of birth?
Or is there a different truth to unearth??
Death and birth are the same, it might be said,
For birth determines an inevitable death.
Does death mean an absolute end?
Or can there be other views to comprehend??
Is death that truth which nothing can ever
surpass?
Or even after death can we take birth?
In the after-world, what determines heaven and
hell?
And is it joy or sorrow that will prevail??
Is the dead's world opposite from where we are?
Or do the dead dwell in many a star??

Do the dead look down to see their loved ones on land?
Or are they emotionless and like a statue do they stand??
What is the truth? Why don't the dead confess?
Are the dead powerful enough to curse or bless??
Where do the souls go after heaving their last breath?
What and where exactly is this world beyond death??

Range O' Orange

Piles of orange leaves raked aside,
Orange leaves on the ground...
Crackling under the happy feet
Of children jumping around...
In the far west peeps the setting sun,
Clad in the silky orange gown...
Painting the clouds with orange paint,
With orange rays bathing the town...
Orange mud tiles that bask in the hue,
Treetops reaching out for the sun,
Orange tint in the autumn breeze
Bidding farewell to the orange bun...

Freckled oranges amidst the lush greens...
Signs of gangrening lives,
Shrivelled up to the very centre,
In their last days trying to survive...
Sunrise in the green, and dusking in orange
To transcend to life anew....

The orange, yet the dawn of what's new to come
Revived by the dawning dew....
Yet, orange like the saffron cloth
Dedicated to the hymns of God...
The yearning to give up earthly life,
To become one with the Lord....

Orange is still that serenity...
If not of life, then of death
And yet, the end of the suffering
Which with life we beget...
And that orange of the flickering flame
Of the raging fire wild...
In the flaming orange, the orange leaves burn,
Leaves and fire both become ashes, into death as they sile..
The green earth formed from an orange ball,
Again into fire will turn,
And the orange ball of restlessness
Into blackness will drown.

Bells

Bells..
Li'l bells..
Tinkling chimes
Silver...sparkling
My own image plays
On their silver bodies
Reminds me of some old dreams
Forgotten.......lost.....and yet vivid
A parting gift, because I thought you loved
Tales....of some long forgotten childhood..

Bells..
Sirens??
Broken dreams,
....Silencing cries..
Yet that undying hope..
You'd come when I call...
someone's hope, for others, a prayer
....Inanimate..........yet owning life.....

For some, they tinkle...for some they sing..
An instrument for safeguarding memories....

Bells..
A voice..
Yours, I think..
Distraught, yet soothes
.....An eternal friend........
Adorning Christmas trees..
.......Creating a symphony...
A mirage perceived by my ears..
......Enlivening our togetherness.....
......Like imaginary fays in my hands......

Emily

The phone rang...
"*Emily?*" He spoke on the receiver....
"*It's a girl*"...she said...
"*Eloise...shall we call her?*"
Teardrops fell...tears of joy...
A smile...a sudden groping for words..
"*Eloise...yes! Yes...lovely name...Eloise..*"
He hardly could speak...
"*Oh! My Emily*"....he had said...

Days passed...and months...

The phone rang...
"*Emily?*" He spoke on the receiver....
"*My duty is over...and I must die,*
Be the shield of my angel...she is not even one."
...Her voice faded, his vision blurred...
Rushing back home, he found her sleeping

On the couch...the baby played, snuggled to her bosom...
Well...she slept...but she did not breathe.
"*Oh! My Emily*"....he had said...

Years passed...and decades...

The phone rang...
"*Em....*"...it was a slip of the tongue...
"*Yes*"...said a voice, ethereal...
"*Eloise is now 31...you can leave her hand,*
And come, walk with me."
His voice choked...and so did his life.
In the office chair he sat,
A body bereft of heartbeat.
"*Oh! My Emily*"....he had said...

Paned

Storms—I saw them clear,
But felt not the wind that blew
To gurgle and whisper to the leaves;
To scare the birds that flew.
Raindrops fell on greying asphalt,
And on passersby scurrying back home,
But never on my draughted face,
Behind the glass pane, I stood alone.

The tempest took over the city-scape,
The mighty trees too surrendered,
Tossed and turned in a midnight storm,
Bruised, hurt, and tender.
It was a cold night; I made a guess,
But feel it? Oh! I could not.
Behind the glass pane alone I stood
Unaware of the cold, and the hot.

The lights mounted on the street lamp poles
Shone like luminescent globes,
Like the headlights of some mail train
Bringing news of despair, life, and hope.
On my glass-pane the raindrops danced
And settled like a million golden dots,
Telling stories of the kindling stars,
And of battles won and lost.

Windows shuddered as the last train rattled past,
On the kohled, damp, mirrory streets
Empty busses, their shadows cast,
Skipping and slipping on the liquid concrete.
I wished…nay! I hoped to do more than see,
But I was statued, unable to move,
Unable to reach my hands out to you,
Unable to heal the gangrening groove.

Strangers came, looked and spoke
Under the sunshade of the bare-bricked homes,
But to them, I was an alien folk,
Like one in a coffin, under a blanket of loam.
I saw, yet I could not comfort
The moaning eyes of the orphaned child,
With nobody to mend his broken heart,
The other kids, drunk on life, continued to play.

I knew I felt the moisture in my eyes,
I knew the fragrance of my garland,
I stood there, a spectre in thin air,
Like washed-out life on the mortal sand.
Caught in the storm of life, chained in fate,
Went unnoticed my eyes of disdain,
Nonexistent, unacknowledged, as a mere portrait
Behind a picture frame I was paned.

A World of Fireflies

Reddening skies and whining breeze
Sodden flower beds and new-washed leaves...
The skies adorned in her cottony gown...
A washed-out moon overlooking the town...
But across the sky they form a shroud...
Fixed are the stars...quavers only the cloud..
A firefly universe, studded everywhere to shimmer..
A twitch....a spark...and a gentle tremor..
A happy-hearted drizzle descending from the blues
A million shooting stars amidst the storm that brews...
An unearthly realm of will-o'-wisps...
Rain drops, like fireflies, seem to frisk...
And yet when rain does cease, it leaves behind its trace

On petals...on eyelashes....and on the leaf blades
Like priceless stones on the soggy mud-beds...
Like glowing gems garlanded in a thread...
Like numerous pearls....lucid....crystal clear..
Like orbs....like dew....like forsaken tears
Like innumerable fireflies on the cold-bodied wire..
Like tiny fragments of love....undying desire...
I lift up my hands and touch the golden glow..
The spheres break...and down they flow...
The fireflies trickle down my hands
Like watery veins surfacing on my skin
Glistening in the escaping light
Shining from the village inn...
Undying fireflies to this mortal eye...
Where fire glows on...yet stars do die....

Eternal Sleep

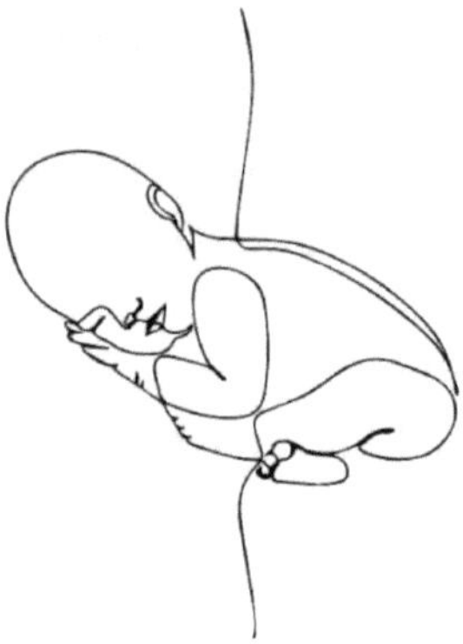

I would meet you....I knew I would....
Finally came that day when at last I could
Finally break apart all those bars....
And travel all that distance across the stars....
I dressed up....like a princess...like the one in thy womb..
Like that little bud you left alone to blossom and to bloom...
I flew right across the soggy greys of dirt galore
I glided amidst the white clouds towards that golden door
Where little angels danced and sang, with indeed no bar of time
Where faded all earthly troubles and the mind moved towards the sublime
And then I witnessed the golden throne on which sat the Christ...

The altar set above the world, even higher than the highest...
Soon enough I found you serving the holy throne
I knew you were divine....and so pure....you were the seed he had sown...
I called out aloud and you came to a halt, your eyes were filled with tears...
And overflowed those feelings that you expressed not for years...
You spread out your loving arms and called me close to you...
To feel that love which once had died, but was now revived anew...
I then knew that success had I gained, and justified why my body I had slain...
I ran towards you, and fell asleep in your arms, never to wake up again...

Fear Just The Fear

What's there to fear when things go wrong??
You can't be weak, you need to be strong.
What's there to fear when you can't do your task??
Smile, it's better than grumbling from dawn to dusk.
What's there to fear when you are in peril??
It's just an obstacle on your way to the top of the hill.
What's there to fear speaking your mind out??
You need not always be a part of the crowd.
What's there to fear when you are in a mess??
Just be brave and fight away your stress.
What's there to fear when people are rude??
Please be stable and fix up your mood.
What's there to fear when you are opposed by your fate??

Be sure to get your success even if it is late.
What’s there to fear if you fall off the peak??
You can climb up again, just don’t be meek.
What’s there to fear if you die tomorrow??
Rejoice, it's the end to all earthly sorrow.
In this entire world, fear not a thing...
‘Cause fear, depression, failure and illness all come in a string.
Be strong and brave enough to fight your way out,
Trust yourself completely and never have a doubt.
Don’t be a living dead till you actually die,
Try, try and simply try.
On Earth, there’s only one enemy in all,
Fear is the only foe that causes man's downfall.
There’s a solution to all problems, just wipe away your tear,
The golden rule to a life worth living is,
"FEAR JUST THE FEAR."

The Death Petition

Facing death in that dungeon cold:
Resisting, fighting…holding onto life,
Fearless eyes shining on the face so bold;
The last attempts to survive…
And in my dreams that maiden I had seen,
Standing, draped in the shroud of fate,
Nine mirrors, and reflections nine…
Waiting to enter the world of death.
With death lurking at her orlay,
She showed no signs to fight,
I let away my own struggle
When I saw her in my insight…
My struggle to live now took a turn,
I now struggled to protect her from dying…
And with this I face death yet again,
This time, prepared to die.

Lord, if this be the taste of death,
I would die a thousand times,
I'd wish for another chance if I could gain,
Not to live, but to re-live
That death again…
As my ice-cold heart grew warmer,
I died in my dreams last summer…

Mother Death

In the cold valley, covered in tranquil snow...
Naked trees helplessly letting go of their last leaves..
A frozen river...the lively brook with lifeless flow,
The living doomed by sterility...yet the dead conceive...
Like carved ice, neither living....nor clinically dead,
She lay there, like an ignorant kid making a snow angel...
Snowflakes on the eyelashes, an invisible halo on the head..
Before the eternal climb, resting at the foot in the deluged dale..
A strange melody of calm...infusing the enchanted air...

The image of your eyes playing in her sleepless eyes...
Like the sails of the homeward boat, your veliferous hair
Fluttering...a woman she perceived in her dreamy surmise..
You walked to her, stroking with your blessing hand,
Whispering some magic words into her snow-kissed ear..
Beneath her ankles, her white gown fanned...
Engulfed by the ambiance of your divinity, bereft of fear...
Rested on your lap that sleepless head of hers...
Her tired soul praying for rest...like an eternal faith...
Shrouded in white....with smiling eyes to bless, to uncurse...
She was allured into the caressing arms of Mother Death...

The Hallowed Hall of Jurisdiction

Rows of benches and a stage to confess,
Where grave decisions are taken for those in distress.
There's the honourable judge to whom people pay reference
And the dragging tedious court case keeps everyone in suspense.
And there stood a youth on whose face was an anxious sorrow,
He was stuck in a case, he wasn't at fault though.
I went up to him and he just heaved a heavy sigh.
I truly felt sorry for him, I cannot deny.
And when to me the entire story was known,
Hatred for the culprit, in me had grown.
I looked around the so-called famous courtroom:
A room filled with sad stories, and infinite gloom.

I then figured out something that was not very strange,
The courtroom's concept remained unaltered, but its appearance changed.
Long ago, even in the age-old ancient days,
People practised the same old judicial ways,
But what abruptly struck my mind
Was that true justice we hardly ever find.
When on the cross Christ was crucified,
A heavy heave of agony, justice had sighed.
During India's freedom struggle, justicc was required,
But on the contrary, the poor Indians were fired.
Death was written in their unlucky fate
Just because "Justice" responded a bit too late.
When the murder case of Arushi was put aside,
It was right inside the courtroom where justice was denied.
Many unfair verdicts in the courtroom are delivered
Which make the life and future of so many innocents blurred.
But it's not in the courtroom where justice we'll find.
It's a person's conscience, justice has to be embedded in the mind.
When the mind is fearless, and the heart is pure,
Justice can be achieved, that is for sure.
I pray, may that man get what is just,

May the word ‘justice’ not break his trust.
May in the courtroom eternal justice occur,
May not the wrong deeds continuously recur.
May it be proved that justice is not a game,
From the hallowed Hall of Jurisdiction,
May the truth always be claimed.

Un- Doubted

Each person is an enemy until he proves to be a friend,
War will persist, until humans want it to end.
Jealousy, fear, agony, anger won't ever cease to exist
Until to end them, we wholeheartedly insist.
Throughout the ages, and even today, people only know to doubt,
They think of only revenge, and venting the venom out.
Only hatred and suspicion are tiring, and disheartening to see,
Innocence, trust, and friendship would be so lovely.
Live a life of values, not just monetary gain,
Let not the poison percolate through each of your veins.

Let go of this negativity, shed the hate that crusts your heart,
Learn to love, learn to trust, live again from the start.
Doubts will leave you nowhere, they will only seize your solace,
Misunderstanding is a curse, quarrel's a disgrace.
Cure your mind of this distrust, try not to fret,
Don't dwell in doubts, cherish the fulfillment you'll get.

The Polestar

I am a little spark
Shining between two glass blue orbs—
Called eyes.
I am like an angel dressed in complete white
Removing darkness from the world and making
it bright.
I am like a tiger and in the jungle I am caged,
And I show you the right path went towards me,
you gazed.
I am royal, glorious, majestic.
I am a prisoner condemned for life.
I am still up there in the night sky,
Trying hard to survive.
Now I might be feeble, like a tiny seed.
Help me grow so that I can help others in need.
I am like all the rest and yet a unique one.
I am the diamond of the night just like during
the day is the sun.
I am a prisoner outside and in.

I am a fire that can never be still,
But I am too feeble, I am burnt.
I shall cremate myself one day;
My ashes buried in your brain.
But from my ashes,
Like a Phoenix I shall rise,
And even after death
In your heart, I shall survive.
To you I shall be very close and yet very far,
To you I shall be one just like the polestar.

The Dancing Fire in Man

Fire, fire, dancing wild,
Raging, and cruel, your mercy is mild.
Your flames flickering to reach great heights,
Your brightness executing your mystic might.
You dance in patterns in your own sway,
And gobble up things that come your way.
You make others surrender to your will,
You are the spirit that can never be still.
You prove your power in every way you can,
You represent the heart of man.
The fire in man helps him strive.
The fire is, but the wavelength of his life,
Your flames flicker and burn, but never give up
hope.
It shows the hardships with which man has to
cope.
When your flames burn, high and low,
It shows that life is a bumpy ride for man to go.

Your restlessness and infinite shape is such,
It blows man's tension and anxiety so much.
The ups and downs of your flames do count
When man faces downfalls, but again tries to
mount
When the wind rises, and the fire is almost dead,
It tells of terrible times that nearly put man on
his deathbed.
Your flame glows on with a mighty will,
Your flames become bleak, yet burn thoroughly
until
A strong gush of wind blows the oxygen out
This gush of wind is now your death, no doubt.
Then man's eyes close forever that day
And the flames of fire also fade away.

Crucifixion of Life

Opening my eyes, I turned around.
I looked everywhere, but nothing was found.
All I felt that environed me
Was a vast darkness, aiming towards infinity.

And all of a sudden, I heard a cry.
The voice was undoubtedly mine, I couldn't
deny.
And the voice, though bleak, sheltered no fear,
And the shrill voice pierced right through my
ear.

As I approached, I found to my disgrace,
In front of me was my own sorrowful face,
And my body was pinned to the cross of the
Lord,
It painted me much more than I could afford.

Upon my head was bestowed the thorny crown,
I saw a teardrop gently rolling down—
As clear as a crystal, smooth like a pearl,
It moistened the cheek as soft as a rose petal.

I saw myself struggling in unseen pain.
I saw me swingeing myself for humanity's gain.
In front of me, my own death. I couldn't bear to see,
So I turned away frantically, trying to flee.

Just then around me, spread a blinding light,
And a glorious scene came into my sight.
From my crucified body, I saw many a glistening ray.
Just then I heard the voice, and it commanded "Stay."

It said, "From here there is no place out and no way in,
To gain actual freedom, you must look within.
When within you seeds of goodness you have sown,
When your heart throbs for others and not for your own,
You'll find that you are one with those few
Whose lives have been proved to be true.
Your body may die, but your soul will not,

And your sacrifice will benefit mankind a lot.
And alive you will be year after year,
And you will inspire others to own a mind without fear.
This will be your goal and your ultimate aim.
You will be the ever-burning, inspiring candle flame.
Through this crucifixion, you won't cease to strive,
Because it is not death; it's the crucifixion of life.

Miles Travelled by a Milestone

I stand upright and sturdy, be it night or day.
I am a milestone embedded on the side of the Broadway
And year after year the right direction I have shown
To those people for whom this place is unknown,
And as I see so many people passing by me,
My old deep-rooted memories forcefully tend to break free.
When my existence came to be, I may not know,
I existed even centuries back, I was not lifeless, though.
I was a banyan tree, tall and huge,
And in me many animals and birds took refuge.
And around me was a city so serene,

All painted in a hue of lush green.
Plassey—I heard, was the name of my town
And King Sirajud Daulah was the man wearing the crown,
But soon my home turned into a battlefield
And I saw people getting ready with swords and shields.
The war that I saw, and the people getting killed
Injured my heart such that I could never be healed.
I froze right there, but Time went on,
I didn't even realise when my life was gone.
And as I watched the extent of inhumanity,
And the several cases of unseen insanity,
I simply hardened both outside and in
And in the form of dust, sadness was accumulating.
I then found that I had become rock-hard, I was then a stone,
And as a fossilised tree trunk, I lay all alone.
Then one day I was chiseled and polished and shaped,
And in the new appearance of a milestone, I was now draped.
I now help the people who go astray.
I steer them back into the right way.
When the cold winds and stony hail hit me seldom,

I quietly think of my years which are yet to
come,
Continuous ruthlessness of the weather will
wear me out,
And I'll take the form of soil without a doubt,
And even then the growth of trees I will nourish,
May I always be helpful, this would be my last
wish.
As a tree, I grew from the soil, and will become
soil myself,
I will become totally one with the place where I
have dwelt.

An Unsung Saga of Love

With a cold heart, the bird lay still,
trying to be nourished by his partner's bill.
It all started when the night had just gone by,
The time when the birds had just begun to fly,
And along with his friend, the man stood with
his gun,
They became ready to shoot the birds just for
fun,
Though at first, they were not favoured by their
luck,
But in the end, quite a few lives were struck.
In the last attempt, the man shot once more,
Bringing down the bird in whose heart love was
stored.
And immersed in darkness, there the bird lay,
Though in the joyful season, in the month of
May,
And it was almost the end of his life,
Yet he tried hard to survive.

And a cry of melancholy was let out by whose partner was dead.
She walked towards him, heartbroken, with a heavy head.
With a cold head, the bird lay still
Trying to be nourished by his partner's bill,
And then the man shot once again,
And with frozen bodies, both the lovers lay on the lane.
That day, the lovers died, but the love did not,
And into the word "love," true eternity they had brought.

Penalty Promulgated For The Peacock's Pride

The story that I am going to narrate
Is about a proud peacock and its fate.
In the jungle it was certainly the prettiest bird
And so, from everyone its praises were heard.
The vibrant colours that played in its many a wing
Made it think that it was the ultimate king.
Its pride had gone above the measurable line
But little did it know that THIS would cause his decline.
It was so overtaken by its pride,
That it forgot what it truly was from inside.
One fine day when the birds had a meet,
The peacock thought that it would be given the highest seat.
And as it was showing off the colours of its wing

Happened the most unpleasant thing.
That day, the hunters had come to shoot their prey,
And saw the peacock's plumage of violet, blue and grey.
After this, all that could be said,
Was that they shot the bird dead.
And there, in front of everyone's sight,
Came an end to the peacock's life and pride.

Fly Little Birdie, Fly

Chirp Chirp Chirp
The little birdie sings.
Flap Flap Flap
She opens out her wings.
Here and there
She peers and sees,
Through the thickets
Of the lovely green trees.
She looks up into
The blue-blue sky
She makes up her mind,
That she has to fly.

9 789363 306363

Printed by Libri Plureos GmbH in Hamburg, Germany